Search!

BY
JAMES R. WARNKE

COVER PHOTO BY
RANDALL JOHN WARNKE

1st Printing May 1982

Updated and Enlarged Edition January 1992
Published by
Warnke Publishing
P.O. Box 1408
Boynton Beach, Florida 33425

ISBN 0-96-31693-0-0

Library of Congress Catalog Card #92-93022

Printed in the United States of America
by Futura Printing, Inc.
Boynton Beach, Florida
33435

TO MY
CHILDREN

BILL
TOM
TERRY
RANDY
WENDY
ANN

AND THEIR
CHILDREN!

— INDEX —

INTRODUCTION

This book on how to search buildings and yards for hidden valuables can also be used as a primer on how to hide things from the prying eyes of the public (or relatives).

Most of us at one time or another in our lives wish to hide away money or other valuables, either for a short time or for the long term. At the same time we want those goodies to be easily accessible when needed. For centuries people from all walks of life have hidden away valuable possessions and then have died without leaving any clues to the secret hiding place.

It is not the purpose of this book to go into the legalities of searching houses, buildings or lands that do not belong to the searcher. Everything in this country belongs to someone, whether it be the government, private individuals or corporations.

I am assuming that when you make use of the tips outlined here you will have full permission to search the premises in which you are interested. The fact that you are fifty miles from the nearest town and run across a hundred year old deserted shack is in no way different than going into an empty house in your town that has not been lived in for twenty-four hours. If you ask permission of the owners and offer to share with them any valuables found, chances are that they will be more than glad to let you search.

Have permission to search. Period. Have you ever tried to

come up with an excuse for trespassing while you are looking down the holes of a double barrel shotgun?

Woe be unto the outsider who is caught trespassing by a small town cop, is hauled before the policeman's brother who is the local Justice of the Peace, is fined and told to pay the clerk of the court who is the wife of the mayor and if no money is forthcoming, might spend a week or so in jail which is run by the policeman who arrested him in the first place! Have permission to search. Period.

Searching buildings and especially the surrounding yards can be done without any physical aids, however shovels, probes, screwdrivers and other tools will greatly help in your quest. To do a very complete examination of every possible hiding place will require the use of a modern electronic metal detector. Millions of people have found a new and fascinating

Abandoned farm machinery.

hobby by using metal detectors to locate money, artifacts and jewelry that would otherwise be forever lost.

If you do not have a detector most cities now have dealers selling them and hundreds of treasure hunting clubs are springing up all over the country. Any of the searchers active in these organizations will be glad to help you or let you know where you may obtain a detector for your own use.

This book is slanted towards those who own and know how to use a modern detector. When it is mentioned "search the edge of the driveway", I mean to use a detector to recover lost coins and rings that might have been dropped there. If you do not have a detector available, most of the hiding places mentioned can be found without using one. If you want to get ideas from this book on where to hide valuables, you don't need an electronic gadget to do so!

Whatever the method of recovery, the search is half the fun. Please be very careful not to destroy any property or leave any holes showing where you have searched. The same principal applies here as with any hobby or outdoor sport. Leave things the same or in better condition than when you found them!

When searching any building, whether it be an old homestead, an abandoned farm, a modern but deserted residence or a prospector's shack, keep one idea in mind. Stop, think, visualize and put yourself into the mind of the former residents. Let me give you an example.

Say you have found a wonderful old farmhouse that you are sure has been vacant for many, many years. You have parked your car in the shade of a huge old oak tree. There is stillness. Perhaps you can hear a few birds chirping nearby while down across the overgrown pasture a squirrel chatters while looking for hickory nuts. The broken windows of the old place stare at you from out of the past. An abandoned hay rake in the side yard overgrown with weeds is a silent reminder of what once was. You can hear distant traffic on the main road but here there is a quietness with a counterpoint of crickets in the deep grass. You came to search, but now is the time to stop, think and visualize.

If you had lived here, were distrustful of banks, needed an ever ready poke of cash, wanted to hide some bills for the coming seed purchases, had a windfall that was better not reported to the IRS, wanted to keep some silver dollars aside for your grandchildren or simply wanted to hide a nest egg . . . you would not, and I repeat, **would not** go out into the middle of a field and bury it. In order to retrieve it you would need some sort of landmark.

The landmarks are what this book is all about. You have to stop, think and visualize what was in the mind of the person that hid the money. Put yourself in his place and, after careful contemplation, start your search.

I have compiled these ideas and tips in this book from many years of personal experience and I am very grateful to those who have helped me over the years by letting me pick their brains, not only in person but through their writings. Carson, Garrett, VonMueller, Marquiss, Hendricks, Evans, Goble, Hemsher, Ballinger, Hertado, Auerbach, Lamme, Dack, Caplinger, Weller, and many, many more.

James R. Warnke
Boynton Beach, Florida
January 1992

LET'S START
AT THE TOP —

Cupola

THE ROOF!

O.K., we are on a site that bears searching. Let's start at the top. It has often been said that the best way in life is to start at the bottom and work up, but in our searches we are going to start at the top . . . if you started at the bottom you might be too tired to search the top and thereby miss some goodies. Several years ago my good friend Bob Goble and I searched an old abandoned church way back in the boonies. We found nothing of interest and being hot and tired we quit and went home. Some months later someone told us that the old bronze church bell had been recovered from the belfry. Start at the top!

The attic you say. Perhaps the rafters. Copper rain gutters

Rafter cubbyholes.

are valuable. No! I mean 'way up on top. Have you recently seen the prices that are being paid for lightning rods and old weather vanes? To say nothing of weatherbeaten cupulas. To put up a ladder and then walk around on top of an old deserted building is to invite broken bones and various other unpleasant happenings. Be careful. A typical brass rooster weather vane will bring over one hundred dollars at an antique shop and lightning rods with purple balls are not far behind that price. The grey and weatherbeaten shingles that you are trodding on are prized by artists who are into painting in the rustic manner. The copper gutters? So far as I know no one is collecting them but the price of copper is going up every day.

So I guess we are through with the roof. Or are we? Did you see the two bricks in the fireplace chimney that looked different? Are they loose? Coins could be hidden behind these loose bricks and they would not be affected by the heat. How about that cupula we mentioned before. Check it out. Not only is it valuable as a primitive antique but it is also an excellent hidey place for valuables that would not be hurt by the weather.

If the house is really falling down check the rafters to see if possibly they are wormwood chesnut or, in the south, pecky cypress. These types of timber are no longer available and are extremely valuable.

CONTINUING
FROM THE TOP —

Nature takes over.

THE ATTIC!

I cannot remember any old building, or modern for that matter, that I have searched that did not contain something in the attic. The attic is the historic place to store any family's past. It is amazing that so many families move away and forget to take the things in the attic with them. OR, they move away and think that the things left in the top of the house are worthless and simply leave them there.

People nowadays are collecting anything. **Anything!** Pick up a copy of the **Collectors News** or the **Antique Trader** and you will find ads from collectors wanting firemen's helmets, old razors, whiffle trees, steamer trunks, fountain pens and Coke bottles. I think that I can make a general statement without rebuttal that anything found in an attic that has not been touched for twenty years has some value to a collector. Orange crate labels, old cigar boxes, comic strips, automobile ads, bubble gum cards, you name it! If you are not sure about something, take it along anyway. You never know.

Now that you have removed the obvious goodies it is time to search further. Look back under the eaves where the roof meets the rafters. Is there a portion of the attic that is blocked off? It may have been an upstairs bedroom for kids many long years ago and then boarded up and forgotten. If so, you have found a bonanza! Old newspapers were used in the past for insulation before fiberglass came on the scene. Historical articles bring a premium from collectors of Americana.

We are now through searching the attic. Are we? Do you see those little spaces between the rafters and the shingles just over the entrance? Check them out for hidden bills and documents. Be sure to look under any insulation or trash right next to the attic entrance. What better place to hide valuables! Folding stairways may conceal folding money taped under the steps. Look!

Attics in most older homes had some sort of floor covering the bare joists, either boards or hardwood strips. Attics were then used to hang up washing on rainy days and many were the coins that fell out of pa's pants pockets to roll into the cracks between the boards. Children have played in attics in inclement days for decades. What did they lose between the cracks or secreted away through the knotholes?

Look around further before leaving the garret. Is there a valuable stained glass or artwork window in the end gables? Are there any old electrical insulators?

Before you leave, look again at that old box in the corner full of old books that the mice have chewed on. The books are worthless, yes, but did you fan the pages to see if there was any paper money hidden there?

No matter how completely you think you might have searched the attic pause, and look again.

100 years of history and artifacts.

THE INTERIOR!

It has been shown many times that most people wanting to hide valuables will choose the interior of a house to secrete them as opposed to outside burial places. There are so many places to hide things within a building that we cannot keep an orderly method of search but must ramble throughout the house and examine everything room by room. Let us assume that the owner of the home had a roll of cash that he wanted to hide. He thought to himself, "I know just the place to squirrel this away where nobody would ever think of looking". And so he did. Years later he went on to that great Treasure House in the Sky and took his secret with him. Let's see if we can find it!

If the house is furnished we will leave those things for later and concentrate on the building itself. Run your hand across the top of every door. A hole might have been drilled into the top to conceal a cache of bills. Are the jambs and moldings tight? Sometimes a molding board is held with only a small nail or two allowing it to be pulled away revealing a small hiding place. If the door is an old type with large keyholes children might have dropped dimes or nickles into the hole. Brass doorknobs and plates are fetching a premium in the antique market and old porcelain knobs are also valuable. Under many doors there is a thin wooden strip holding linoleum or carpeting in place but might also conceal a cavity for money. Most interior doors are hollow and a small slit may have been cut near the top to receive coins. Why anyone would choose this method to hide coins is beyond me as the only way to retrieve the money would be to tear the door apart, but it has been known to have been done!

Baseboards. Most moldings along the bottoms of walls are held in place and trimmed with what is known as quarter

Hidden doorway.

round. This thin strip is supposed to be tight against the floor but usually has a small gap due to warping or shrinkage. Over many, many years of sweeping the floors a lot of coins such as silver dimes and quarters end up hidden under the trim. Although not exactly a hiding place, these cracks could yield a lot of valuable coins. Loose baseboards have been known to conceal valuables, however the chances are slim to find anything there . . . or is that what the hider was thinking?

Many older homes were heated with a huge furnace in the basement and the hot air was fed to the first floor rooms by means of floor openings called ducts. Most of us in our September years can remember standing in our pajamas over these ducts while hot air warmed our bottoms on a cold winter morning. These ducts or registers may hold many coins lost over the years. Removing the wooden or metal screen from the open-

Coffee can bank.

ing was easy and may have been the hiding place for grandma's egg money. In any case, search the interior of all duct-work. Coins, earrings or toys may have been hidden there or just lost.

In July of 1981 in Boynton Beach, Florida, a student was attending classes in a temporary trailer when he lost his pencil down an air conditioning duct. Reaching in to search for it he came up with a fistful of $100 bills. As of this writing the student, the school officials, the teacher, the former trailer owner, the present trailer owner and the city are all interested in the treasure trove. The case is going to end up in court and the winners, of course, will be the various lawyers involved.

Window sills are removable and then can be replaced with only a nail or two holding them in place. What a bank! Many of the girls in the old western houses of ill fame hid a few high graded dollars away from the possessive madam. Many an old timer thought the cavity under the window sill was the ideal place for his hidden treasures. Many a modern drug dealer thinks that no one (except you and I) would ever look for his cash under a window sill. Anytime I enter a building to search for treasures I always check the window sills and the surrounding framework. Several years ago a friend of mine and I were exploring a deserted house near Grant, Florida. We found a lot of old newspapers that had historic interest and also a lot of old housewares to sell at the local flea market. He asked me to take a picture of him standing in the tumbled down doorway. Before I could snap the shot he pulled at the window frame next to the door and found a Bull Durham sack with twenty old silver dollars. Can you blame us if we forgot to take any more pictures?

Is there a stairway going to the second or third floor? It has been found that most people hiding things favored the first step, however any of the treads could be loosened for a deposit area. Check them all. The newel post at the end of the bannister sometimes could be unscrewed revealing the hollow interior of the post itself. This hidden bank was especially

Old newspapers can be valuable.

used during the Civil War era. We don't find many modern houses with "unscrewable" newel posts, but it is a point to keep in mind while searching any old building or deserted homestead. The space under the stairs was very often used as a storage closet. After thoroughly checking this area stop and think. Does the closet encompass the entire area under the stairs? Or is there a small area blocked off under the last tread that could be a hideyhole? Look under each tread for money that could have been taped or stapled there. Look back and see if there is anything hidden over the small doorway. This has always been a favorite spot to secrete a bag of coins or a roll of cash. One of my treasure hunting partners found a box under a staircase filled with jars of figs put up by the housewife fifty years ago. The figs were very, very putrid but the jars were very, very rare and brought a good price at the local antique shop.

The walls of any house or building do not lend themselves very well as hiding places but there are some places that should not be overlooked. In any room that had a wood stove there will be a round hole near the ceiling for the stovepipe. These holes were usually covered with a decorative tin plate that snapped in place over the hole when the pipe was removed in the summertime. Not only are these plates now collector's items but the cavity behind them is an ideal hiding place.

Search window frames.

Cash in top of door.

Examine all mopboards and molding trim for loose sections held in place by only a small nail or two. Check all electrical outlets and switches for money hidden behind their covers. This idea for a hiding place is not new and many mail order catalogs today are advertising false electrical receptacles to be inserted into the wall as a small safe.

If you are lucky enough to be in a house that is to be torn down and the owner doesn't care if you wreck things by all means tear apart some of the wallboards or paneling to see what they conceal. The present wall coverings may have been built over and covered up some very old and interesting wallpaper or newspapers used for insulation. In an old tumbled down shack in Colorado I found the inside of the wall boards to be covered with newspapers dating back to the 1800's. Not much intrinsic value but certainly interesting! A treasure hunter in Arizona got a metal detector reading from the wall of an old house much louder than the small signals of the usual nails holding the wall together. When the boards were pryed away he was the proud new owner of a 1873 Winchester carbine. He was about to quit and call it a day but wisely decided to check the area again with the detector and got another strong signal. This time it was an old canvas bag with ammunitition for the rifle and ten silver dollars. You never know!

Remember the old cowboy and Indian movies wherein the homesteader hustled his wife and children down into a room under the floor through a trapdoor concealed normally by a rug while he fought off the Indians? Those hidden doors did exist and it is a very good idea to pull back any floor covering and check for them. Stamp on the floor and listen for hollow sounds different from the rest of the deck. New flooring might have been laid that would have covered up the old trapdoor. We have to remember, especially in very old buildings, that the residents of that era did not have access to a nearby bank to deposit their funds. They had to conceal all valuables somewhere and we, the searchers, have to think of every available place where they might have hidden those treasures.

Bathrooms. For some reason or other bathrooms have been the hiding place for many caches of money and jewelry. Perhaps the person sitting there has more time to contemplate on where to hide things. Plastic bags of money have been found in many a water tank behind the toilet. In older houses there was an overhead tank that was flushed with a pull chain. Not only was this a ready made bank but the old wooden tank itself is now prized by collectors. People have been known to drop coins into the razor blade slot of the medicine cabinet every time they shaved. Rather a weird idea, but it has been done and after that person passed on who would think of looking there? Look under the sink for money taped there and check for the same thing behind the toilet tank. Outhouses? We will get to them later.

Do the outside measurements match the interior size?

Closets have been the natural storage places for every family and are used for everything from coats, Christmas presents and shoes to hidden valuables. When a family moved they cleaned the closets out . . . they thought. They may have missed Aunt Mable's small jewelry box on the back of the top shelf that she hid there before she died ten years ago. They probably did not check under the shelves where they rested on the supporting strips of wood. Five twenty dollar bills were found recently under the edges of a shelf in a house that was going to be torn down. Here again check for loose baseboards and possible cavities under the floor. Some closets had a false wall in the back that opened up to reveal small shelves between the studs. I can remember when I was a kid in Wisconsin that the old house we rented had such a closet with a false door in the back. I hid various coins and toys there and when we moved I forgot all about them. Were they ever found? Along this line it might pay to squat down on the floor and get a child's view of the house. Where would be a good hiding place from that angle?

Take a note pad and measure the outside dimensions of the house. Then measure the size of each of the rooms. Allow for normal thickenesses of the walls and see if your figures are reasonably close. There may be a hidden room or closet that would never be discovered except for your careful measurements. People add on, cover up, remodel and otherwise change houses over the years. I explored an old house in Key West years ago and was puzzled by a walled off section of one of the first floor rooms. With the owner's enthusiastic help I pryed some of the boards loose and we found a hidden stairway to the upstairs. The top of the stairway was boarded up at the back of an added on closet. Present residents were using an outside stairs and had no idea that the old access to the second floor existed. The walls were covered with decorative cloth dating to the 1850's and the stairs were littered with trash now known as antiques. You never know!

Old news may be good news.

FIREPLACES!

Fireplaces have been installed in homes for centuries. For centuries people have been using them for hiding places. It has always been traditional to place a coin under the hearth or the chimney for good luck while the fireplace was being constructed. Usually it was a silver coin in use at the time, however for super good luck, gold coins were better. As you drive today through parts of Georgia and the Carolinas you will be sure to see lone chimneys sticking up in the corn and cotton fields. These are grim monuments to the war when brother fought brother and Sherman made his infamous and firey march to the sea. Most of these brick and stone relics of the past have coins buried under them and the old foundations of the houses that were burned held their own treasures.

Fireplace mantels were sometimes loose so that valuables could be concealed underneath. Ditto for loose bricks within the fire area and surrounding supports. Some fireplaces had an outside access hole with a cover under the fire box so that ashes could be removed without messing up the house. Because these ash removal holes were not subject to very much heat they were ideal places to store the family goodies. It doesn't take much imagination to picture the residents fleeing from the advanced armies and leaving the heirlooms behind in their haste and never being able to return. The same scenario holds true for the old homesteads of the west. Additional note: Have you priced what old fireplace andirons are bringing today in the antique market?

Traditionally, the builder put a coin under the hearthstone for good luck. Care to excavate?

Look everywhere!

BASEMENTS!

When I grew up in Wisconsin every home had a basement. Where I am living now in South Florida, few dwellings have one due to the high water table. BUT, no matter where you live most older homes have some sort of space under the structure. In the north they are basements and in the south they are called crawl spaces. No matter what you call them, these areas have been almost universally used as a repository for yesterday's junk, now known an antiques. Bottles, fishing gear, old lumber, car parts, garden tools, jars of preserves, old stoves, ancient radios, perhaps phonographs and in many, many cases hidden valuables. Perhaps no other place has been used so frequently to secrete money and jewelry.

Basements and other openings under old houses have long held a special fascination for me along with generations of treasure seekers. When I was about twelve years old and living in Fort Atkinson, Wisconsin, the old homestead next to our house was torn down. After the workers left for the day the main building had been removed but the old floor remained which covered the basement. They had nailed the trapdoor shut which led into the cellar but they failed to secure the outside batwing doors. What kids at that age can resist exploring a spooky cavern? Three of us in the evening crept into the forbidden basement with candles and matches not knowing what we would find and scared of what we might. It was sort of a let down after we bravely told each other, "Shucks, I'm not

Crawl space

scared, let's look around." There wasn't much to see, no skeletons, no treasure chests or ghosts. What we did see were shelves lining the walls loaded with old dishes, cut glass, ancient picture frames, some rusty iron toys and funny looking kitchen utensils. We got bored and went home to listen to Amos and Andy and the next day a bulldozer filled in the hole.

I have paid for many an exploration trip by selling artifacts found under houses to antique dealers. Years ago I had special permission to search the oldest house on Duval Street in Key West. (It is not the oldest house still there, but I don't like to disillusion the historians who think so.) This ancient structure had a crawl space, so with a flashlight I crept under the old timbers. I swept cobwebs out of the way and moved old lumber until I was just under the middle of the 150 year old house. The flooring was held up by huge stones and one of them had an inscription. A gravestone had been used as part of the foundation! Just ahead of me there was an old box on its' side and I moved it to see what it contained. With a nasty snarl a huge cat took off under the flooring, and I swear it is true, I went backwards about six feet without moving a muscle. When I calmed down I resumed the search and ended up with some very nice valuable canning jars and a few old coins.

Modern basements have cement block walls, poured reinforced concrete floors, an oil burner humming quietly behind a facade of birch paneling, ping pong tables and the other accoutrements that speak of Suburbia. But the old basements, ah yes, the old basements. Dirt floors, stone walls, an ancient furnace with octopus-like heating pipes, a water heater with it's coils within the furnace grates, coal bin, spiders, paint cans, old stone crocks, cellar bugs, jars of preserves and a single fly specked overhead light bulb. And a smell of the past . . . a certain, dusty, damp smell that is slightly repulsive and yet brings nostalgic memories of our childhood.

Exploring an old cellar is spooky and fun. There are usually antiques to be had but we are mainly concerned with finding any valuables that might have been hidden there. Look up

A bottle bonanza.

and carefully examine all of the beams overhead and the criss-cross boards. Where the ends of the beams rest on the cellar walls there is usually a space that is ideal for small packets or cans. A friend of mine in Georgia found an oilcloth wrapped package filled with confederate bills in one of those overhead crevices. He was about to give them away when he checked with a local dealer and found out that many of the old bills were very valuable to collectors. He was smarter than I was back in the nineteen forties. I was paid a couple of dollars by an old woman to clean out her cellar and put the trash out on the curb to be collected the next day. I remember thinking at the time that she sure hung on to a lot of stuff over the years as most of the bundles I hauled out were magazines dating back to 1900 and boxes of old legal records and letters. It is to cry remembering!

Examine everything very carefully in an old basement. People had a way of concealing cash in the bottom of nail kegs and other containers. Look for loose stones or bricks in the walls. The back floor or wall of a coal bin was a favorite place to hide valuables. A separate room may have been partitioned off as a storage place for preserves. Not only may the jars be valuable but look behind them for envelopes of cash. My father and I explored an old basement in Milwakee and found a room full of dusty bottles filled with homemade grape wine. A bonanza we thought! We started pulling corks and sampling. Vinegar. Every one of those jugs had been filled with wine and loving care years before but over a couple of decades the contents had reverted to a very bad grade of vinegar. After all the bottles were removed from the shelves we found several small books which had no particular value but when the pages were riffled a twenty dollar bill was found that evidently had been used as a bookmark.

The dirt floor (if it is a really old house) is best searched with a metal detector that will discriminate between trash and coins. The detector will find any buried treasure in a hurry and save the work of probing or digging up most of the floor. Use

This fertilizer bag contained no bull!

the detector on the walls as well. Someone may have hidden cash there so long ago that the foundation stones and mortar look the same as the rest of the wall and only a detector will find it for you.

Most basements had workbenches. Those old tools rusting in a corner may have some value. Certain types of wood planes, axes, hammers, wrenches marked "Ford", and specialty tools such as hog ring pliers, nail pullers and draw knives are eagerly sought by collectors of antique tools. It is better to take them along and decide on the value later than to leave them in the dust and regret it!

As I said, basements are spooky and fun but they are also usually a source of many treasures if you know what to look for and what may be valuable.

Mason jar deposit box.

Many homes were built off the ground to avoid frequent flooding in the rainy season.

Watch out for spiders!

**To completely search a yard a modern
detector is a necessity.**

Modern detector prices range from $250 to $1000.

FURNISHINGS!

How many old houses have had all the furnishings removed after the owner died and the resulting truckload of belongings were then taken to the local charity shop or the dump? Perhaps, if the relatives were a little bit smart, they had an auction or called in the used furniture dealer to take the lot for one low price. If they were a little bit smarter, and the house was old, they let the antique shops make bids. If they were super smart they **searched** the furniture and belongings before they did any of the above!

No one can count the number of places there are in any house to hide valuables. The total must run into the hundreds. I am going to list the most obvious places and also many that are **not ever** thought of by those searching or hiding. You must let your imagination run wild. We have all read newspaper stories of someone buying an old chair at the flea market for five dollars and finding a roll of bills in the lining. We have also read many times of an old recluse dying and the police finding thousands of dollars under his mattress or inside his pillow. These places, of course, are very obvious and yet many of those old pillows and mattresses have been dumped without anyone thinking of searching them.

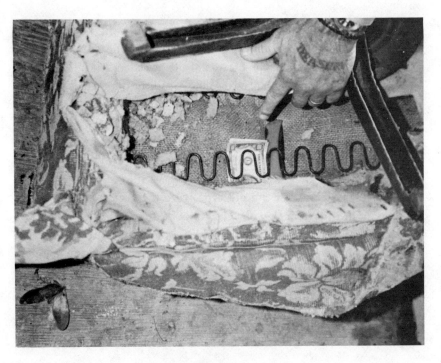

Money under the chair.

Flower pots are a favorite spot for coins and jewels. What better place than under a flowering plant? No one would suspect that there is more in the bottom of the pot than dirt and gravel. Many hiders merely placed a cache of bills under a large planter as a home grown safe.

Picture frames have been a favorite place for large bills for decades. It is so easy to slip money behind Uncle Gustoff's picture and no one will ever know that it is there. Have you looked behind your uncle's picture lately?

Most clocks of the old type have a removable back with enough room for jewelry or bills. Some old alarm clocks had two large bells on top. What better place to roll up some large denomination bills and tape them there under the gongs. Not only does this method mute a strident morning call but every morning the hider is assured that his money is still there.

Expensive fertilizer.

I know of one case where an old Seth Thomas clock had faithfully chimed the hours for many years. When the clock finally gave in to the ravages of time and chimed no more it was taken to the local clock shop for repairs. The repairman not only fixed the clock but was honest enough to tell the owners about a large bundle of gold back bills inside.

You must condition yourself to look **under** things. Check the bottom of every lamp, lantern, ornate jar, planter, shelf, chair, bookcase, waste basket, woodbox, birdcage and stove. For some reason those who want to hide something think first of putting away valuables **under** some familiar object. This instinct must be a throwback to our possible animal heritage . . . dogs bury bones, squirrels dig holes for nuts and pack rats hide anything shiny under their nests. Let us leave this theory to the Darwin types. The fact remains, look under things!

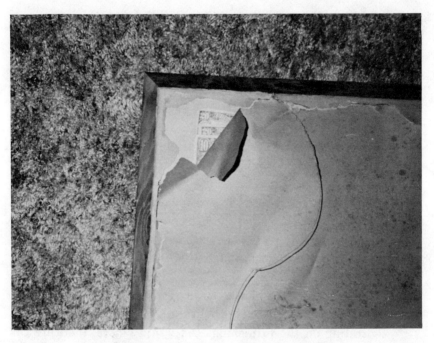

Picture frames — a popular hiding place.

Books and bookcases are hotspots. Thousands of people have hidden money in books. They make a note of the volume, either in writing or mentally, and then unexpectantly pass on to visit with their ancestors. The point is, **never** throw out or give away any book without riffling the pages for hidden money, antique book marks or old letters with valuable stamps. Think about it!

The interior of books may be hollowed out for a hiding place. There are false books on the market today that look like any other book but in reality they are a safe complete with a lock. Bookcases sometimes have false backs. Check everything. You never know.

Let's roam the house you are searching. I am assuming that you have completed the house search and now you are concentrating on the furnishings. As I said before, there are so many places to look it would be impossible to list everything so let's just roam and keep your imagination working!

Book safes can be homemade or purchased.

There have been so many TV shows showing this hiding place that it is hardly worth mentioning. A stash of coins or jewelry inside the toilet tank. I mentioned this place before, but how about things taped under the tank and out of sight? Or an envelope hung behind the water tank? Or bills carefully taped to the underside of the cover? I heard of one case where someone actually removed the float, inserted bills of a large demonation and then soldered it together again. There are wacky manufacturers in this country of ours that fabricate toilet seats out of clear plastic with dozens of coins imbedded within for the ultimate throne. A couple of years ago one of those throne builders ordered several bags of bright new pennies and dimes. At the time he did not know that one bag contained many rare new coins by mistake and they were subsequently buried in several plastic seats. A search ensued for those valuable seats through the retailers but all had been sold. Someone out there may have enough hindsight to spot those coins!

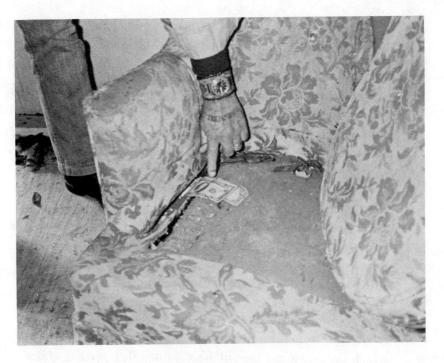

Under the cushion cash.

Pianos have lift-up tops with a large space for goodies and many musical instruments have small holes or compartments to hide money. The sound boxes of guitars, violins and banjos come to mind. Check the bottoms of all drawers for taped envelopes of cash and if there are still dishes on the shelves, don't forget the sugarbowl!

Look in the bottom of sewing baskets and in the back of sewing machine drawers. Check the insides of stuffed animals and the hollow in the bottom of figurines and statues. The list could go on almost forever. Back in the 1930's almost everyone was paid in cash and what wasn't put in the bank had to be kept in a secret place somewhere in the house until it was time to do the weekly shopping on Saturday night. In rare cases surprisingly large sums were hidden by those who didn't trust banks or were too far from town to make deposits. At some time in their lives I am convinced that at least ninety-five percent of our population has hidden money or jewels, either temporarily or as a permanent cache. I have . . . haven't you?

Have you looked everywhere?

Chandeliers are not only possible antiques themselves but also a good place to conceal money. Although you are not very likely to find them, guns have been used as hiding places. Tightly rolled bills can be shoved down barrels and stock butt plates removed to hide jewels. Hidden compartments in old dressers and desks are more common than most people imagine. Use the same method here as you did for the house and check inside and outside dimensions to see if they are within reason. (Customs officials are the experts at this!) There may also be secret compartments in suitcases and old trunks and, of course, any old trunk you might find has good value to the antique buff.

Since this book was first published our country, unfortunately, has been overwhelmed by drug crimes. Almost every day the papers report arrests, either by the local police or by the agents of the border patrols and Coast Guard. The hundreds of places these drugs have been hidden are clues to also searching homes and yards for more mundane types of treasure. Large caches of drug money are found every day by the authorities. If you, in your searches, happen to come across a large amount of modern money you will have to decide what to do. Police? Keep it? Hide it in a different place? I am not going to advise you! I **know** what I would do. (See the chapter on What To Do With What You Find.)

A sewing box may hide Aunt Millie's mad money.

Flashlight bank.

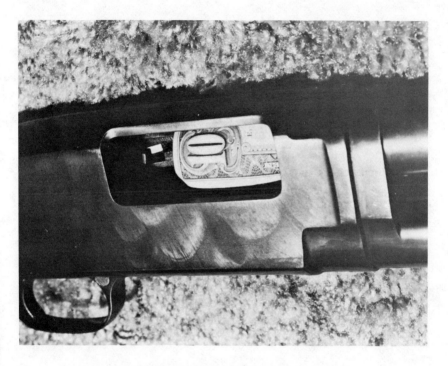

A loaded gun that was not dangerous.

A friend of mine told me the following story and therein lies a lesson for all of us. His father had died a few years before and the family was worried and puzzled about where he had kept his money. Every month he would go into town and cash his social security check and buy a few groceries and pay the utility bills. They were certain that he never spent more than half of his income and yet no cash was found in the house after he passed away except for a few bills in his wallet. The relatives searched every conceivable place in the old homestead and found nothing. They gave up the search and recently my friend went out to the house to do some maintenance work prior to putting it up for sale. He was out in the yard taking pictures for the realty company when he noticed a faint path leading to the back of the lot.

Look under all drawers.

He knew there was an old trash dump back there that had not been used for years and he wondered why there should be a trail into the bushes. He walked the short ways to the overgrown dump pit and the faint pathway ended at the rusted remains of an old Ford. The rusty door opened surprisingly easily and he looked inside. Cobwebs, dust and the musty smell of rotten upholstery greeted him. He turned to leave when he saw the glove compartment had a new hasp and padlock attached! With pounding heart he raced back to his car, grabbed a tire iron and returned to pry open the rusty glove compartment door. There was over $4500 in cash in plastic bags inside.

Which brings us to the next phase of our search . . . the outside yard.

Teddy bear treasure.

THE YARD!

Once again we are standing outside of the house and wondering where the former residents may have hidden something of value. It is quiet, we can still hear the faraway purr of cars on the highway. The crickets have given up to the heat of the day but the long tremulous song of a cicada takes us back to the carefree summers of our childhood. A dog on the next farm is barking incessantly for some reason known only to dogs and a woodpecker is rapping on the leaning telephone pole in the backyard. The muffled roar of a jet overhead breaks our reverie. Up there the stewardesses are serving plastic lunches . . . down here we have a yard to search!

Do you have permission to search?

To thoroughly search any yard you need a modern metal detector. Many hiding places can be found without such a tool but in the long run and to do a complete job a detector is a necessity. As we go over the many places where goodies might be hidden you will see the reason. A cheap detector will have you digging up trash all day while a modern discriminating machine will separate the good from the bad. If you do not have a detector do not be discouraged! There are many, many places to find valuables in any yard without one. A good detector is the frosting on the cake! To illustrate . . .

See that big old oak tree in the frontyard with the remanants of a child's swing hanging from the lower branch? For decades generations of kids played on that swing and lost coins from their pockets in the process. Coins, you say? Why would anyone want to spend time searching for coins dropped from kid's pockets? Pre-1965 dimes and quarters are now selling for five times their face value. Indian head pennies are gaining in price and V-type nickels are collector's items. Silver dollars are wonderful finds, of course. Be sure to check all dates for rarities.

Clothesline poles are good landmarks.

If the yard you are investigating dates back to the 1800's as an occupied place you could find a few coins that would more than pay for your detector. That same oak tree (or maple or elm) is also a landmark. Remember that I mentioned that no one ever buries anything of value without some kind of reference point so that he might find it again? Search carefully around the base of the tree and check to see if there is any hole or opening to a hollow interior where Grandpa Jones might have hidden his silver dollars.

Any other play area in the yard is worth detecting such as under swing sets or jungle gyms. Picnic tables are a good location as is the area around bar-b-que pits. Check very carefully around the base of the bar-b-que grill itself as this could be an ideal landmark. Look for loose stones that can be removed easily. Under the hearth itself loose bricks might cover a secret place.

Look around the base of the flagpole, if there was one. Check also the ground around the mailbox area. It has been the custom for years, and still is, to leave change in the mailbox to purchase stamps from the mailman. Many an old coin dropped there is just under the grass for you to find.

Grandpa may have buried gold coins here.

The edges of the driveway can be especially productive for finding old coins. Everytime someone would reach into his or her pocket for the car keys they might have lost a coin or two.

Are there wooden front steps leading up to the porch? Each lower corner of the steps would be a good place to hide a canning jar full of silver dollars. Don't forget to check the underside of the steps for envelopes of money and then go under the porch itself. If the old porch is the typical wooden type with cracks between the boards, how many coins were lost through the gaps in the flooring? If money were buried there it would probably be as safe as in any bank. An explorer out in Ouray, Colorado found such a porch with a crawl space underneath and as he did not have a detector he carefully measured the distances from corner to corner. Finding the exact center of the dirt under the porch he dug and found a rusty metal box full of silver dollars. He never revealed just how much he found, but he sure didn't have to worry about grocery prices for quite a while!

Steps to a forgotten past.

Every house before the coming of the electric dryer had a clothesline. Many were the pants that were hung upside down on those lines and had forgotten coins fall into the grass beneath for the present day searcher to find. The area around the base of the clothespoles was also used as a landmark for buried treasures.

Have you ever heard of a posthole bank? Your ancestors did. This method of concealing valuables has been used for centuries and is still rather common today. The farmer would go out into his back yard and pick one of his fenceposts as **the marker** for his bank. Perhaps it would be the fifth one counting from the corner of the barn. It may have been the southeast corner post of the vegetable garden or maybe the left hand post supporting the stile. (Ask your grandpa what a stile is if you are fortunate enough to be young enough not to know!)

Any corner may be a "posthole bank".

At the base of the selected post he would dig a hole and carefully bury cash or other valuables in a sealed container such as a canning jar or tobacco can. Such a posthole bank probably would have been fairly close to the house for convenience sake and also within view of the owner. It will only take a few minutes for you to check every post within reasonable distance of the homestead. While checking the fenceline watch for posts that are capped with tin cans. Posts tend to rot out quickly on top and it was (and still is) a common practice to put old cans over the top of the posts to prevent deterioration. **Also,** holes could have been drilled into the top of the posts, money concealed there and then covered with an empty Arbuckle can. (Ask your Grandpa about that one, too!) While checking the fence lines of very old farms you may come across some odd looking barbed wire. There are many barbed wire collectors today who will pay for old and especially rare sections of those thorny strands.

Hollow trees may have hidden treasure — and wasps!

Outhouses (and you don't have to ask grandpa to know what I am talking about now) probably are the best places in the whole yard to look for yesteryear's treasures. Because they were private places and could be visited frequently without arousing suspicion, they were also used for making deposits of the money variety. Small openings where the roof joined the wall were ideal for hiding cash and loose floorboards covered many a can full of jewels. The outside corners of the privy were also used as landmarks for buried valuables. The box holding the toilet paper or cobs could be a door to a hidden compartment. After searching everything else, take a look at the flooring. Are the boards separated by cracks? How many coins might lie underneath those planks that fell from the pockets of hastily pulled down pants? Although we are trying to find treasures purposely hidden let me add the following tip. The pit under the seats of old outhouses was a favorite place to dispose of empty poison bottles and forbidden (by grandma) whiskey flasks. Over the years everything in the outhouse pit of offensive nature has long since decomposed into plain soil. Digging there today would be no more repulsive than spading your garden and the bottles to be found are true antiques and valuable.

Deposits in this primitive bank may also
have been of the cash variety.

Is there a birdbath in the yard? It may be sitting on top of a hidden cache, of course, but birdbaths come apart and most posts holding the bath part are hollow. After looking under the bath check the inside, too. Brass sundials set on top of small concrete pillars may conceal a hollow time capsule, so to speak.

Statuary in an old yard, if someone hasn't swiped them, may cover a stash in the ground. What better landmark? Most statues are hollow and are ideal for oilcloth wrapped treasures. I know of one treasure hunter who had an old cannon in his front yard for a decoration and kept plastic wrapped extra funds hidden by shoving the cache down the barrel. To retrieve the cache he used a fishhook taped to the end of a stick to pull the package out. (He told me that when he retrieved the money he "always got a charge out of it!".) Sorry about that.

Money has been found in very strange places.

Under a bird bath.

A telephone terminal cache.

Search under all landmarks.

In the midwestern part of our country most homesteads had storm cellars in the back yard for a retreat in case of tornados. Remember Dorothy's farm in the Wizard of Oz? These dugouts with big flap type doors were also a favorite place to keep family treasures. Some doubled as cool cellars for preserves and barrels of apples and potatoes. Here again, as we did in the cellar of the main house, check under, around and behind everything. Go over the floor, which was usually dirt, with your detector and check the walls for loose bricks or stones. The outside corners of the storm cellar are also landmarks.

Kids loved to play in the spooky storm cellar caves and probably lost coins in the process. Grandpa may have used the cool recesses for stashing his booze or hiding money. Exploring abandoned storm cellars today can be rewarding, but watch out for snakes, scorpions, spiders and the owner if you do not have his permission to search!

The old folks at home have long since been buried.

What pioneer family did this fireplace keep warm 75 years ago?

Cisterns. Sometimes these holders of rainwater were outside and covered with cement slabs and other times they were a separate room in the basement. A pipe then led to the large handled pump in the yard or to a pitcher pump in the kitchen. The cisterns were supplied by downspouts from the eaves-troughs on the edges of the roof of the house. What a wonderful place to hide money! A zinc topped canning jar could be filled with cash and lowered with a string to the bottom of the water. A whole (let us dream for a moment) treasure chest could have been thrown into the water for safe-keeping. How to search a cistern? With difficulty. If it is dry there is no problem, but if it is still full of stagnant and scummy water you have a problem of the first magnitude. (Definition of first magnitude: Darn near impossible!) I have used a very strong magnet to drag the bottom of filled cisterns and a large three pronged fish hook can be used as an improvised grappling hook. If you have a strong suspicion that there might be something really valuable hidden there you might have to devise a way to drain the tank.

A pump may remain on top of an old cistern.

Five centuries ago the indians of Yucatan used their wells, called cenotes, as receptacles for offerings to the gods. A hundred and twenty years in the past wells were utilized for the quick storage of family silverplate due to the threat of the invasion of the Army of the Potomac into the plantations of our beloved South. The pioneers of the far west also thought of the wells when they had to quickly hide valuables from the possible plundering of the indians who were only trying to protect their native lands from the intrusion of the white man. A small stage company was trying to establish a line through the plains and asked the indian guides how far it was from Wichita to the next spring so that they could set up a waystation. The indians replied in broken English, "Wells far-go". Anyway . . . that's the story I got of how the famous name originated!

These old bricks were part of a wellhouse foundation.

Wells can and do hold vast amounts of treasure. They also hold many bodies of various animals that have fallen into the openings and have died there for want of a way to get out. Old wells are dangerous! Most of them were built of bricks in sort of a bottle shape with a wide bottom and narrow top. They were covered with a sturdy wooden platform which held the pump. Over the years this plank covering would rot and become unable to either hold up the pump or the weight of anyone walking over it. Be extremely careful exploring near old well sites. If you plan to go down into the well make sure you have someone on the surface to rescue you. I know from experience that you will probably need assistance to get out.

The best way to search an old well is the same method used in cisterns. Use a heavy magnet or some sort of grappling hook. If the well you find is dry you are twice blessed . . . once for finding someone's ideal hiding place and secondly for the insatiable urge to explore it's interiors. I am assuming that you are an intelligent adult, have a good buddy standing by with ropes, that there is no methane gas in the well, that you have permission to search the property, that you have at least one spare flashlight, that you have a sufficient supply of snake bite anti-venom on hand, that you are not afraid of spiders, that rotting animal carcasses don't bother you and that you have said all of the prayers taught to you in your childhood. **Then,** my friend, descend into that old well!

A gazebo.

Have you ever heard of a gazebo? They were small covered bench areas, usually near or in a garden, that were used by the owners for quietly sitting and contemplating nature or something. In any case, they were ideal landmarks and deserve a careful search under, in and around.

Windmills used to dot our rural countryside before the advent of electric lines. The legs of the high towers were usually set into concrete pilings level with the ground and, of course, are obvious places to search. There is at least one authenticated case on record of a man finding a sealed can of coins inside the gear box at the top of an old windmill. These structures should be climbed with caution because most of them found today are about ready to fall down at the slightest excuse. The water pump at the base of the windmill is a collector's item today as well as the windmill blades.

A wishing well.

The mug is worth more than the contents!

Loose bricks may indicate a hidey-hole.

How many coins beneath the old park bench?

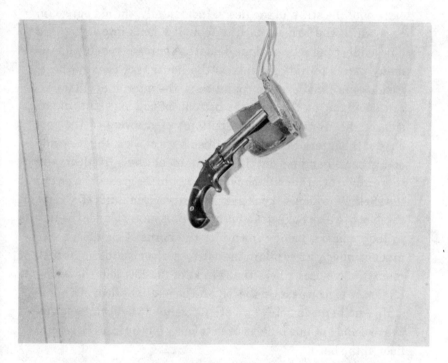

An 1860 .22 pistol found by a magnet lowered into an old well.

All outbuildings are worthy of thoughtful examination. Chicken coops have been known to hide many a monetary nest egg under the straw of the nests. Incidentally, the old porcelain eggs which the farmers used to fool slow hens into laying are now avidly sought by antique dealers. A garage probably has as many places to hide goodies as the house. Look everywhere. Inside cans of nails, under paint cans, the interior of old inner-tubes hanging on the wall, the bottoms of nail kegs, the underside of the work bench, the bottoms of drawers of the tool chests, the interior of partially filled bags of seed, the backside of hubcaps hanging on the wall, under the dirt floor and there might even be coins shoved down into the grease can on the top shelf. Who knows. Look everywhere you can think of. Everything above also holds true for barns plus more. Under the hay in the mangers, money sewn into the horns of saddles, boxes hidden under a straw pile in the loft, loose floor boards in the tack room, the crevices where the rafters of the roof join the walls, under the pigeon nests in the loft and beneath the floor of a horse stall. Another side note . . . check for valuable lightning rods on the roof and antique pulleys used to carry hay up into the second floor of the barn.

Old pennies behind the fuses may be collector items.

Outside again and continuing. Houses covered with clapboard siding have been known to have a loose board easily removed revealing a hiding place. Each corner of a garden could be a landmark as well as the corners of any building or foundation. Check the base of each tree in the orchard. Perhaps the hider counted out three trees to the north and two to the west for his secret place. If there is a woodpile I would have to say . . . maybe. Anyone wishing to conceal money would have to go to a lot of work to move a woodpile, bury his cash and then replace the wood. But it is possible.

Look back at the house from a different angle and think some more. Are there shutters? Do they have a false back? How about that outside fuse box. Remember when the fuse would blow and someone would put a penny behind the fuse for a temporary repair? Old pennies are getting more valuable every day. The dog house! What better place to conceal money than under Fido's home. Check for any loose bricks in the back of the chimney. Look for any landmarks you might have missed the first time around. Everything has now been checked out.

A metal detector will find many old coins in the yard.

No! Remember the story I told you relating to the path leading to the old dump and the car? Where I grew up in southern Wisconsin many year ago every farm had a large pit somewhere on the premises that was used for dumping trash. The old saying is "yesterday's trash is tomorrow's treasure". While not a likely place for hiding valuables, these old dumps contain a fantastic amount of things that are considered antiques today. Candle molds, kerosene lamps, coal scuttles, chinaware, milk cans, iron frying pans, dutch ovens, Mason jars, wine bottles, you name it! If you are lucky enough to find one of these old dumps that has not been used for decades, set aside two or three day's time to explore its' depths and you will be richly rewarded.

One farmer in Indiana, realizing people were interested in his huge old dump site, actually charged antique buffs by the hour for digging privileges.

Most cities no longer allow scavengers in their dumps because of liability risks, however old abandoned dump sites can be antique gold mines such as the one in Leadville, Colorado.

The thrill of old gold and the agony of the I.R.S.

The search ideas in this book have been mostly slanted towards farms and homesteads, however the principals apply to modern homes as well. Have you ever heard someone say "well, we cleaned out Aunt Bessie's apartment and finally got rid of all that junk!" I can remember very well when I have helped some of my relatives clean house after a death. Looking back now I can't help think about some of the treasures we threw away and the many hiding places we did not search.

Now for the obvious question. Where would I hide money if I did not have a bank available? I really don't know for sure but one idea comes to mind. Instead of a money belt make up a money collar and put it around the neck of a very mean Doberman. Place the dog inside of a yard surrounded with an eight foot high chain link fence with barbed wire on top. Post a large sign on the fence that reads "Warning! This yard is protected by an electric fence and a man with a double barrel shotgun three nights a week. You guess the night!"

100 years ago children played here — and lost coins.

Out buildings are favorite landmarks.

WHAT TO DO WITH WHAT YOU FIND!

Treasure trove laws have 50 different versions in the 50 states of our United States. Whatever you find, whether it is jewelry, money, stocks, antiques or old coins, belongs or did belong to someone.

The old saying "finders keeprs, losers weepers" simply does not apply in most cases.

Let us look at a hypothetical case. You find an abandoned homestead miles from anywhere and you search the interior of the old house. You find a hidden cache of old and rare gold coins behind the false wall of the upstairs closet. Elated, you pocket them, run for the car and head to the local coin shop to see how much they are worth.

"How about these beauties, Jake," you say.

"Those are really excellent rare coins, Jim," Jake replies. "I'll give you $4500 for them today but the market is going down and I can't offer that price tomorrow."

Still elated with your luck you decide to take his generous offer. Jake is curious.

"Tell me, Jim. Where did you find these lovelies?"

"Remember the old Johnson homestead five miles off the main road?" you reply. "The place is falling down and I found these coins behind the upstairs closet. Don't tell anybody, but I plan to go out there again on Tuesday and see if there is anything more to be found."

Jake sure does remember and Monday finds him out at the old Johnson place along with some of his friends. On Tuesday half the town is ransacking the old homestead. On Wednesday the owners of the property have gotten word of the treasure trove and have contacted the attorneys for the estate. On Thursday Jim has been arrested for trespassing and the police arrest Jake for receiving stolen property. On Friday Jim is out of jail on $10,000 bond and has had to hire an expensive lawyer. Jake is released because he is the cousin of the County Judge.

Does this sound far fetched? This scenario may be a little fast, but the basic lesson is there. Be sure you have permission to search. If the owners of the property don't care and give you carte blanche you have it made. If they are reluctant to let you do your thing, get an agreement in writing before searching. Most agreements between owners and the treasure hunter specify a fifty-fifty split of anything found of value. This is only fair.

The second lesson to be gained from my little story is to keep your mouth shut. Period. Be sure you are legal in what you are doing. Be fair to everyone concerned. Respect the rights of others. Do not destroy property. Keep your mouth shut. Period.

With all of the above in mind, let's get back to the original question. What do do with what you find.

COINS!

Coin dealers have to make a profit and most of the coins they buy they must keep in stock until they find a buyer willing to give them a price that will result in a profit. Therefore most dealers will offer about half of what the book price calls for. Your local library has the latest coin price books which you should consult before accepting any offer from a dealer or anyone else. In case you are lucky enough to find really rare and valuable coins you should probably hold on to them. The market in rarities has never gone down and they are a good investment for the future.

Never try to clean old coins if you think they may have numismatic value. An excellent find in like new condition can have it's value drastically reduced by rubbing it with any type of cleanser. It is far better to take it to a reliable coin expert for evaluation before any type of cleaning.

FOR INFORMATION ON COIN VALUES:

COIN PRICES
NUMISMATIC NEWS
700 E. State St., Iola, WI 54990

COINAGE MAGAZINE
2660 E. Main St., Ventura, CA 93003

PRICE GUIDE OF US COINS (known as the Blackbook)
The House of Collectables, 201 E. 50th St., New York, NY 10022

GRADING STANDARD FOR US COINS
THE NUMISMATIST
American Numismatic Assoc., 818 N. Cascade Ave., Colorado
Springs, CO 80903

HANDBOOK OF US COINS (known as the Redbook)
Western Publishing Co., Racine, WI 53404

COIN WORLD
GUIDE TO US COINS, PRICES AND VALUE TRENDS
Amos Press, P.O. Box 150, Sidney, OH 45367

The above publications and many others are probably available in your library or can be purchased at coin dealers and newstands.

Wicker furniture is in great demand by antique dealers.

ANTIQUES!

Old items from our past have never been in such great demand as they are today. The preceding paragraph on coins also holds true for antiques. Dealers can only offer about half of what your oldies are worth. Auction houses may bring you a tremendous price or you might get stung. Advertise your finds in the local paper and see if you can attract good buyers. Put your valuables on consignment in the local antique shop. Be cagey. You know what you have to offer and let buyers come to you.

Antiques and collectibles price lists are accurate for one, perhaps two years. Inflation, changing collector interest, current events and dwindling supplies influence the market. Prices do not rise in an orderly manner. The following price guides can help you establish the value of your finds:

Kovel's Antiques and Collectibles Price List, 50,000 current prices. 782 pages. $10.95. P.O. Box 22200-P, Beachwood, OH 44122

Official Identification and Price Guide to Antiques and Collectables, $12.95. 1086 pages. House of Collectables, NY

Antique Trader Antiques and Collectables Price Guide, $12.95. Babka, Dubuque, IA 52001

Warman's Antiques and Their Prices, $13.95. 709 pages. Wallace-Homestead, Radnor, PA 19087

Flea Market Trader, $9.95. 319 pages. Collector Books, Paducah, KY 42003

See your local library for sample copies and exact addresses.

STOCKS AND BONDS!

An original issue of the Ford Motor Company is worth a fortune today. The first stock certificates issued for Jones Gold Mining Co. are worthless. Never, and I repeat, never throw away any certificate until you have researched them for possible value. Even though the stock has been cancelled there are many collectors who are interested in and active in scripophily, which refers to the collecting of antique stock and bond certificates.

Most old certificates have no face value but almost **all** of them are worth from $1 to $5000 to serious collectors. Rarity is the best indicator of value, but I repeat . . . any cancelled stock certificate will be worth from $1 up to a collector.

Jones Gold Mining stock is worthless on the New York stock exchange but the document itself may be the nest egg you have been looking for.

To determine if the uncancelled certificate you have found in the bottom of an old trunk in the attic has any value ask any major securities firm to look up the company name in their copies of Standard and Poor's or Moody's old corporate records. If the stock has been cancelled, that is paid off, a dealer specializing in old stock certificates would be glad to appraise it for you. In either case, don't be in a hurry to sell. It always is prudent to get second and third opinions.

The good, the bad and the valuable!

OTHER THINGS FOUND!

Go to your local antique shop and ask to see a copy of the Collector's News or the Antique Trader. You will be absolutely amazed at the tremendous variety of items that people collect. Antiques in the past had to be at least 100 years old before they could be called antique. Times have changed. I bought my first television set in 1950 for $250. It was an 8" Hallicrafters black and white. Today the same set in working condition is worth $1000. What do you have in your garage that is only thirty-two years old and worth four times what you paid for it? Think about it! The best way to get familiar with the prices today is to visit your nearest flea market on the week-end and see what your recovered items are bringing on the open market. Be sensible, be wise, be honest, make sure that you are right, and then go ahead!

Finding is half the fun!

RECENT FINDS REPORTED!

California. A woman cleaning her attic found a well worn letter dated Nov. 16, 1862 and signed by Abraham Lincoln. Latest bids have reached $65,000.

Austria. In 1938 a wealthy Austrian named Rudolf Seidler escaped to the United States with his family. Before he left he secreted his valuables in two different places. Part of his hoard was placed in a new electric stove and discovered by workmen in 1954. The other half he had placed inside a 1937 Electra vacuum cleaner and this portion is still missing.

Cleveland, OH. An elderly recluse died in 1970. When his house was demolished the ruins revealed $100,000 in $10 to $100 bills.

West Medford, MA. A fire gutted part of the home of a retired attorney. Firemen were helping to clean up the mess when they discovered coins and securities worth over $250,000. A wooden chest half full of silver coins and over $6000 worth of dimes was discovered under a stairway. A tree had grown up blocking the garage door and inside was a 1934 Ford in almost new condition and worth $50,000. After the 86 year old owner was taken to a local hospital his nephew hired an armored car to transport the coins and securities to a bank in Boston.

Chicago, IL. The old home of "Garbage Granny" was the site of a frantic treasure hunt recently when a bulldozer digging a foundation nearby uncovered several silver dollars. A young boy, using a metal detector, found many dollars of historic value while the 'dozer operator continued and dug up a quart Mason jar full of silver dollars. He took the jar and left the job.

Waterloo, IA. A district court judge ruled recently that a plumber could keep the $2700 he found in a home where he was working. He had been sent to remodel a bathroom and while tearing out the wall behind the bathtub he found a can containing the money in old bills. The owner laid claim to the cache, but the judge ruled that he could not prove rightful ownership and awarded the treasure trove to the finder.

Long Island, NY. Two young men aged 14 were exploring a deserted beach cottage in 1979. The crawl space under the house fascinated the boys because of the abandoned fishing gear and boxes stored there. They found a plastic bag containing $50,000 in small bills. Local authorities took charge of the money until the rightful owners come forth, but they think the cash will be given to the boys eventually as the police determined it is probably drug related.

Columbus, OH. Pre-1900 silver dollars and over 400 old silver dimes were found in the basement of a lived in home. The owner was checking some wiring along the ceiling next to the cement block wall and found the money in a jar. He had no idea who hid the money there or when.

Richmond, VA. A couple got a big surprise when they inspected the insulation of their home and found $300,000 in small bills. The former owner was a wealthy bailbondsman who had died in 1978. The finders, with tremendous honesty, contacted the estate of the deceased millionaire.

Harrisburg, Arkansas. A man searching an old farmhouse was about to throw away a coldcream jar partially filled but decided to clean it out anyway. There was a five dollar gold piece in the bottom under the cream.

LaCrosse, WI. Four teenagers were hired to do some digging under a 120 year old home to make a space for new heating ducts. They saw a kettle on top of a brick wall but ignored it until it was time to take the wall down and then they looked inside the old pot. They found a cache of $5, $10 and $20 U.S. gold coins dating from 1870 to 1893. The face value came to $14,000 but worth much more to coin collectors.

Fountain Valley, CA. A woman held a garage sale and sold her green sweatshirt for $2. She later remembered she had put a small pouch containing four diamond and sapphire rings and a diamond pendant in a pocket of the suit. The jewelry was valued at about $10,000 and she had no idea who the customer was.

New Orleans, LA. A backhoe excavating an old bank site unearthed two 10 by 12 by 8 inch wooden boxes that broke open spilling a hoard of gold and silver coins. Over 200 bystanders rushed into the muck to grab for the money. The fabulous cache included quarters from the New Orleans mint in the early 1840's, Spanish coins from the middle 1700's and Mexican coins. Many of the valuable coins were probably not recovered from the sticky clay although the search continued for two days.

Baltimore, MD. A man withdrew $1200 from his bank and hid the money from burglars in a pair of shoes. He later threw the shoes out. After notifying the trash company he spent two hours at the dump and finally found his shoes with the money intact. He said later, "I'll still hide my money in shoes because a mattress gets lumpy with money inside."

Louisville, KY. Two sacks of mail that should have been delivered in 1910 were found in an old house and turned over to the Postal Service for a very late delivery. A family found the sacks while remodeling an old home that had once been the local post office. The bags contained over 500 pieces of mail including 1910 seed catalogs, flyers for a clothing sale and some first class letters.

Valhalla, NY. A check for $25,000 was found by a woman who purchased items sold for unclaimed storage. The check was hidden between the pages of a book and was dated 1950. The old check made out to Marguerite Haymes . . . also known as Rita Hayworth . . . had an illegible signature.

Ft. Worth, TX. A billfold that had been missing for 25 years was found behind a wall in the old Turrant County Courthouse. The wallet was owned by a woman who had died three years earlier.

Austin, TX. A woman was panic-stricken when she realized that she had left $4000 worth of valuables stashed in a fake beer can on a Port Aransas beach. She had hidden the jewelry and cash in an imitation Miller Lite can and put it in the family's bar refrigerator while they went on a trip. Her husband mistook the can for the real thing and took it along. Later, when he couldn't get the can open, he threw it away on the beach. Two boys found it, unscrewed the cap and discovered the valuable contents. They took it to the police. The woman called the police later and asked where trash was taken from the beach and explained what happened. The police told her they had the can and she picked it up. The two honest boys were rewarded.

Sanford, FL. A woman who had hid $8000 worth of jewels in one of her son's jigsaw-puzzle boxes discovered he had given the game to a charity and the charity had thrown it away. She said most of it was covered by insurance but the insurance company would probably cancel her policy for being so careless.

Fruitland Park, FL. Firefighters put out a fire in an old eccentric's home and found him dead in a chair. Also in the rubble were found six metal cans filled with gold and silver coins that he had hidden. The neighbors had thought that he was very poor.

New York, NY. Sotheby's auctioned off nearly two million dollars worth of the late Andy Warhol's jewelry. Later, while moving two file cabinets, the workers found even a greater amount of valuables hidden in false-bottom drawers. This fortune in jewelry and watches were also auctioned to benefit the Andy Warhol Foundation.

New York, NY. The United States Banker magazine has estimated that there is $3.3 billion dollars hidden in secret places.

Boston, MA. A couple bought a valuable 1780 Chippendale desk and discovered a secret compartment. Inside was a note reading, "I found it first! 1922."

Peoria, IL. A man's father, who had been an avid amateur photographer, died. While cleaning out the darkroom and packing up the chemicals he noticed one can was very heavy. Opening it, he found over $8000 in face value of old gold and silver coins. The man and his mother had no idea that the father was secretly collecting old coins.

Somewhere in the northeast. A couple bought a vacation home and while his wife cleaned the kitchen, the husband started on the fireplace. When he dislodged the flue to take it outside for cleaning, out tumbled bundles of brownpaper wrapped rolls of bills, $50's and $100's. The total came to over $500,000. They searched the rest of the cottage and could find no other papers such as wills and documents. The couple wish to remain anonymous because of possible connections to a drug deal and have retained a lawyer to work with the IRS.

Chicago, IL. A real estate agent held a sale of the contents of a home that had been vacant for two years. Unable to sell a 1950 era gas stove he dismantled it to make it easier to haul away and found a small box containing $15,000. The seller's mother had apparently hidden the money before she died. The agent called the seller and returned the money.

Philadelphia, PA. A woman withdrew $2000 from the bank thinking that the bank was close to going under. She put the money in an envelope and hid it in a wastebasket. It slipped her mind and the basket was emptied into the garbage. The money was never recovered.

New York, NY. Two sanitation workers found a bundle of cash in a barrel and turned in the $48,900. They got a thank you, that's all. The authorities said they were not entitled to any of the loot which consisted of 410 $100 bills and 158 $50 bills neatly bound with rubber bands and hidden in a Queens alley.

Brighton, NY. A woman hid her family jewels in a cookie tin and then sold the tin at a garage sale for 10 cents.

Washington, DC. Anyone who has found mutilated money or damaged it themselves can probably get some restitution from the Govt. Experts in the Office of Currency Standards have reconstructed bills that have been mutilated in a blender, scrubbed in washing machines, poached in a waterbed and, in one case, eaten by a cow. As long as they can put together at least fifty percent of a damaged bill they will refund the full amount to the owner. They tell people not to microwave wet bills as they will dry naturally enough but crumble when touched. For information write to the Dept. of the Treasury, Bureau of Engraving and Printing, OCS, Room 344 BEPA, P.O. Box 37048, Washington, DC 20013.

Aurora, NY. A man who died in 1917 told his son that he had hidden treasure on his property but did not reveal the location. The son searched for 70 years but never found the cache. A few years later the son's widow hired workmen to renovate the 140 year old house overlooking Cayuga Lake in upstate New York. The workmen found a hidden room containing an 1856 Mason jar and a cork lined wine decanter holding more than 200 coins including two three cent coins from 1869 worth $700 apiece, an 1855 Half Anna, indian-head coins and women's rights currency dated 1879.

Jackson, TN. Workmen resurfacing a parking lot uncovered a trove of U.S. gold coins worth up to $3000 each and made off with them before the police could seal off the area. The Mayor said that somebody probably buried them in 1861 or 1862 to hide the coins from the advancing federal troops.

Pembroke Pines, FL. A city maintenance worker was astounded to see $20,500 worth of bonds, traveler's checks and cashier's checks fall from a pile of trash he was dumping. He took the trove to his boss who then called the owner. She said that apparently her late husband had hidden the items in a false bottom of a kitchen cabinet without telling her. When she remodeled the kitchen and threw out the old cabinets the valuables surfaced in the workmen's trash truck.

Washington, PA. An 89 year old recluse froze to death after ordering his gas service cut off two years before. Neighbors called the police when they noticed a door open and the man was found fully clothed and dead in his bed. After a search, authorities discovered $188,000 in cash hidden in an unlocked safe, a steel box under the bed and another steel box under the sitting room.

Waco, TX. A contractor won a contract to remove the metal from several old houses that were to be demolished. When he took down a lead downspout a large leather bag fell out spilling gold coins dating back to the 1830's with an estimated value of $130,000.

Jupiter, FL. A hermit living on 300 acres along the Loxahatchee River died and for several years treasure hunters searched for his hidden money. The State of Florida acquired the land and closed the property to the public. Two rangers were restoring the boards around the fireplace of the recluse's cabin and found a hidden slot in the chimney containing 5000 coins with a face value of $1829.

Fort Lauderdale, FL. Workmen using a bulldozer were razing an old apartment building when the blade struck a planter on the front porch and $2500 worth of old silver dollars, quarters and dimes poured out. The owner said he had no idea who buried the money and allowed the workers to keep it.

Manistee, MI. Over $900 in old large type currency was found in the overhead rafters in the attic of a 90 year old home. The money was stashed in a very rusty lard can.

Atlantic, IA. $190 in misc. gold coins were found in an iron cannister. The container was buried in a pig pen which, at one time, was the location of a chicken coop.

All of these fascinating tales are true! They have been gleaned from news articles in the media during the period 1980 through 1990 and are on file. How many thousands more were never reported?

The above finds are not unusual. They are happening every day around the world. Most recoveries, for obvious reasons, are never reported to the press or the police. It is almost a universal human trait, sometimes called the squirrel syndrome, to hide away something of value for the future. During the past decade many alarmists have been advocating buying bags of silver coins, acquiring gold Krugerands, putting in stocks of freeze dried foods and otherwise preparing for the coming crash of our society as we know it. They may be right, I don't know. What I do know is that there is a tremendous amount of treasure hidden in homes and yards across the United States for you to find. Why not try it?

YOU AND THE LAW, GOOD LUCK!

Years ago when I tried to get a lease to look for sunken treasure near one of our southern states I was told to first contribute several thousand dollars to the governor's campaign fund. Years ago treasure hunters were classed in the same category by the public as surfers, skin divers and and motorcyclists. Those other hobbies are now respectable and accepted and treasure hunting is enjoyed by millions of us folks. We seem to be accepted by everyone except the politicians. With a few exceptions they know nothing about our hobby, but instead listen to desk-bound historians and archaeological professors who get sick at the mention of treasure hunters.

I would like to pass on a few quotes from actual letters from various state officials in our "land of the free". In most cases they have no idea of what we are trying to accomplish and have very closed minds about what the treasure hunting fraternity can contribute to our nation's history. All of the following quotes apply to treasure hunting on state lands.

ARIZONA: "If treasure were found on state lands it would be **state property** and subject to state disposition."

CALIFORNIA: "Metal detectors may be used only to detect modern day coins. Persons uncovering any other material while using a metal detector within a state beach area are asked to leave the material in place and immediately **advise an employee of the find and it's location.**"

FLORIDA: ". . . we do discourage the use of metal detectors since there is really **nothing to be gained.**"

GEORGIA: "It shall be unlawful for any person to use or **possess** in any park or historic site any electronic device for the detection of metals, minerals, artifacts, lost articles or for any treasure hunting."

HAWAII: **"We do not have any restrictions** against the use of metal detectors within our state parks."

IDAHO: "Visitors at Idaho State Parks may not dig or disturb the park premises, however one might use a metal detector **without digging**."

INDIANA: "The lost and found valuables, including archaeological artifacts, **must be turned in** to the park manager for proper disposal."

MONTANA: "No person shall disturb or remove the **topsoil cover.** This prohibits digging for worms, burying of garbage and allowing pets to dig holes."

NEW HAMPSHIRE: "Anything found on state lands belongs to the state. Money or items valued in excess of $5 are to be **reported to the park manager.**"

TEXAS: "No person shall operate or otherwise use a metal detector in any unit of the state park system except for the **employees of the Department.**"

WASHINGTON: "Digging in any soil, earth or on any beach is prohibited. Use of a metal detector would be **closely scrutinized** by the park manager, since the logical act after finding an object would be to **dig for it.**"

UNITED STATES DEPARTMENT OF THE INTERIOR: "The use of metal detectors is specifically prohibited. The resources should be conserved by such means as will **leave them unimpaired** for the enjoyment of future generations."

There are many, many other examples of such laws all across the country. Let me ask you, if you found a twenty dollar gold piece in a remote corner of a National Forest would you run to the nearest park ranger and give it to him?

I know of no federal, state or local governments that actively pursue a search for artifacts by the use of metal detectors. Enjoyment for future generations? How in the world can the artifacts be enjoyed if someone doesn't dig them up for museum display?

Did you know that Fort Ticonderoga and Monticello are privately owned? When I approached the managers with a proposal that strictly supervised metal detector users be allowed to find artifacts for their museums do you know what they said? "We have had digs by the universities and perhaps in the future they might find some more things for us." The dozens of trenches and breastworks surrounding Fort Ti will probably never be searched in our lifetime.

During the past few years I have visited the Custer Battlefield, Civil War sites, National Monuments, historical buildings and various battlefields. At no time did I see any government activity to recover artifacts "for the enjoyment of future generations." The area managers seemed to concentrate on well kept lawns and nice flower gardens. One prime example was the Confederate prison camp site of Andersonville. Thirty thousand men and women were kept there on just a few acres during the Civil War. The few extremely interesting artifacts on display are housed in a small and cramped museum. Thousands of more fantastic artifacts are lying under the beautiful lawns "unimpaired."

Treasure hunting is fun. To find long lost articles gives us a thrill even if it is only a belt buckle or a button. To find coins we can sell to help pay for our equipment is a means to an end.

Let us hope that some day government officials will realize what we can offer in the way of locating items that will be lost forever without the help of dedicated explorers. The resurrection of the past can never be accomplished unless they allow us to do so.

The treasure trove and metal detecting laws of Federal, State and some local governments change almost yearly. Some unthinking people over the years have spoiled it for the rest of the responsible hobbyists. They dig up lawns and parks, litter and otherwise create nuisances that provoke officials to make rules and laws prohibiting metal detecting. Please be responsible and treat all property as if it were your own. Some laws are so strict that the police will confiscate your equipment and car if you violate the rules. Be sure you know the laws in your area before enjoying this wonderful hobby.

TREASURE HUNTER'S
CODE OF ETHICS

I WILL respect private property and do no treasure hunting without the owner's permission.

I WILL fill **all** excavations.

I WILL appreciate and protect our heritage of natural resources, wildlife and private property.

I WILL use thoughtfulness, consideration and courtesy at all times.

I WILL build fires in designated or safe places only.

I WILL leave gates as found.

I WILL NOT destroy property, buildings, or what is left of ghost towns and deserted structures.

I WILL NOT tamper with signs, structural facilities or equipment.

I WILL NOT litter.

MORE HIDING PLACES!

Squirrels do it. Pack rats do it. People do it. No, I'm not talking about THAT! You know I am referring to hiding valuables away from predators, both animal and human.

It would be impossible to list all of the hiding places our fertile imaginations can dream up. The following ideas came from readers of the first edition who wrote and said, "Why didn't you tell about . . ." or thoughts that came to me later or related by friends and enemies.

Inside the cardboard tube holding paper towels.

In the kitchen among cooking utensils.

In children's rooms where burglars don't expect things to be hidden.

In fake wall sockets.

In the bottom of a clothes hamper.

Frozen in an ice cube tray.

A phony air conditioning or heating vent.

Put paint in an empty mayonnaise jar, shake it up and

drain the excess paint. When dry use it as a cache in the fridge.

A trap door under the kittylitter box.

In a paper bag on the floor of a clothes closet.

Under the cover of a doorbell.

Open a coffee can from the bottom. When placed back on the shelf rightside up valuables can be hidden underneath.

Behind canned goods in the pantry.

In the bottom of an empty picnic basket covered with a tablecloth.

In the bottom of a box under the workbench with old rags on top.

In the back of an old black and white TV set stored in the basement.

In the bottom of a plastic bag of grass seed.

Sew the ends of the sleeves of an old shirt together and use sleeves for a hiding place.

Put money in a plastic bag and hide in the zippered cushion of lawn furniture.

Hide in a box on a closet shelf and mark it "clothing".

Inside the bag in a broken vacuum cleaner.

Under a stack of towels in the linen closet.

Wrapped in an old sheet in the bottom of a clothes hamper.

Under winter clothing in a box with moth balls.

In the toes of stored work boots.

Inside of an empty cereal box on a kitchen shelf.

Inside of a vase filled with decorative marbles or sand.

Concealed in the hems of drapes. (also some folks put firecrackers in drape hems as a fire alarm.)

Inside the light in the bottom of a ceiling fan.

Under a rug with a piece of heavy furniture on top.

Many mail order catalogs today list hiding cans with screwtop covers that are exact replicas of real items like motor oil, soup, soft drinks, hollow books, beer and insect spray. The smart burglar knows about them and will check them for valuables.

Critics will say that the ideas and thoughts in this book are foolish and that those who want to keep their valuables away from loss due to burglars, fire, etc. should rent a safety deposit box. I AGREE! However, human nature is a funny thing and people will hide away treasures anyway regardless of sensible advice. I have, haven't you?

WALKING FOR TREASURE!

As you and I get on in years, physical activities become more and more something we **should** do rather than what we **want** to do. The doctor tells us to get more exercise. Our spouses call us couch potatoes. Some of us who used to be avid golfers walking the course now rely on carts to do the work. The thought of jogging immediately brings to mind a quiet nap instead. Long walks are O.K. but get boring after awhile. Even our president recently shouted, "Get out there and do something!" I have found my own solution to this problem of geriatric malaise. I do a lot of walking, quite a bit of bending over or stooping and come home with free money and sometimes jewelry! It's called metal detecting or, as some prefer, treasure hunting.

Metal detecting originated before World War II as a military necessity to find mines the enemy had laid in the path of advancing ground forces. The first machines were very cumbersome with a heavy backpack and a long rod and a huge coil to sweep the ground. These early instruments detected all metal and could not tell the difference between a buried beer can and a deadly mine. Today's sophisticated detectors can ignore trash such as nails, pulltabs and bottle caps and let you know when you have found a "good target." They will not only tell you the denomination of the coin hidden beneath the surface but also how deep it is!

You probably have seen detectorists swinging a strange looking coil over the ground in parks, beaches and playgrounds and have wondered what "that nut" was doing. Well, "that nut" was finding coins, car keys, small toys, watches and an occasional piece of gold or silver jewelry. That modern day treasure hunter is getting fresh air, exercise **and**, on an average two hour hunt, has recovered at least three or four dollars in change and perhaps a gold class ring.

How do you get started in this fascinating outdoor hobby? There are tens of thousands of metal detecting enthusiasts across our nation and hundreds of treasure hunting clubs. In your yellow pages you will find dealers listed under "metal detectors." Newspapers will sometimes run notices of local club meetings. Your local Chamber of Commerce probably lists the metal detecting clubs along with the officers to contact.

The cost? Modern metal detectors are not cheap. Those advertised in some discount stores as "treasure finders" selling for about $45 are, in my opinion, a waste of good money. They will find a quarter an inch deep, but that's about it for these cheap machines and the beginner will only become frustrated and disappointed. There are dozens of good modern detectors on the market ranging in price from $200 up to $900. Large magazine stands sell several magazines devoted to the hobby along with ads by the major detector manufacturing companies that will give you an idea of the wide range of machines available. Dealers will be listed and they will be very glad to help you get started with advice and demonstrations of the detectors they have in stock.

How are they used? A metal detector sends an electronic wave or signal through the coil on the end of a shaft into the ground and reads the signal coming back. When the field of the signal is disturbed by a metal object in the ground the detector responds with an audio tone and, in some machines, by indicating on a meter or computer screen what it "thinks" the object may be and it's depth. The operator then carefully digs for the object and retrieves it. Every detector comes with a complete instruc-

The results of one afternoon's search!

tion manual and some companies even provide a video tape on how to use it to your best advantage. There are also several books devoted entirely to the successful use of metal detectors.

The term "treasure hunting" usually brings to mind visions of macho stalwarts hunting for buried chests of gold coins or intrepid divers salvaging Spanish galleons. Such hunting still takes place, especially along the coasts of Florida, but thousands of detector users do their own type of modern treasure hunting in parks, playgrounds, beaches and other areas where large numbers of people gather. They get lots of fresh air and exercise along with the fun of finding what other people have lost. Many grandparents take along the kids and let them have the fun of digging up coins as some older folks may not be able to kneel down too well. No other hobby combines a healthy outdoor activity with free money, jewelry and valuables! Try it!

Beaches hide hundreds of coins and valuable jewelry!

OTHERS WHO MIGHT BENEFIT FROM THIS BOOK!

Insurance adjusters looking for lost or hidden items while adjusting a claim.

Attorneys settling an estate when the heirs think more valuables might be hidden.

House wrecking companies tearing down old houses.

Bulldozer operators grading land around homesteads.

Survey crews who might run across old dumps and wells.

Sellers of old homes and farms.

Buyers of old homes and farms.

Landscaping crews replacing lawns or plants.

Electricians opening up old walls.

Plumbers working in walls and basements.

Air conditioning crews working in attics.

Weekend and professional treasure hunters.

AND, OF COURSE, BURGLARS!

FOR ADDITIONAL INFORMATION!

The information given on the following pages is as accurate as possible as of January 1, 1992.

SOME PUBLICATIONS DIRECTLY RELATED TO TREASURE HUNTING, METAL DETECTORS AND SEARCHING.

Western and Eastern Treasures
5440 Ericson Way
Arcata, CA 95521
(707) 822-8442

Lost Treasure
Treasure Facts
P.O. Box 1589
Grove, OK 74344
(918) 786-2182
FAX (918) 786-2192

Treasure
Treasure Found
31970 Yucaipa Blvd.
Yucaipa, CA 92399
(800) 545-9364

The Treasure Hunter's Express
210 N. Main St.
Ames, NE 38621
(402) 721-8588

Plus Ultra (Spanish Coins and Wrecks)
P.O. Box 1697
West Palm Beach, FL 33402

In The Steps
P.O. Box 910
Hatch, NM 87937

Hundreds of treasure related books have been published over the past thirty years. Those that are classics and the new ones are listed in many ads in the magazines listed or see the appropriate section in your local library.

LOOK FOR THE OBVIOUS!

THINK LIKE THE HIDER!

HAVE PATIENCE!

KEEP LOOKING!

And PLEASE . . .
do not destroy property!

It is impossible to list all of the available hiding places for valuables within houses and the surrounding yards. I have strived with the help of many other people to tell you about as many as possible. I welcome your thoughts and ideas so when this book is revised your suggestions can be included and credited.

Jim Warnke
P.O. Box 1408
Boynton Beach, FL
33425